VOICES INTERNATIO
P R E S

The High Price
I Had To Pay 2

SENTENCED TO 30 YEARS AS A NON-VIOLENT, FIRST TIME OFFENDER

A MEMOIR

MICHELLE MILES

FOREWORD BY JAMILA T. DAVIS

VOICES
INTERNATIONAL PUBLICATIONS

The High Price I Had To Pay: Sentenced To 30 Years In Prison As A First Time, Non-Violent Offender, Volume II

© 2013 by Michelle Miles

This book is a real-life story about the events that led to the imprisonment of author Michelle Miles. All names and events are true. The information in this book can be verified through public record. (See United States v. Miles Docket # CR-97-998 (RJD), U.S. District Court, Eastern District of New York.)

Printed in the United States
First Printing 2013

ISBN: 978-09911041-0-9
LCCN: 2013919024

Voices International Publications Inc.
196-03 Linden Blvd.
St. Albans, NY 11412
"Changing Lives One Page At A Time."
www.voicesbooks.com

Edited by: Jamila T. Davis
Typesetting by: Jana Rade www.impactstudioonline.com
Cover Design by: Keith Saunders www.mariondesigns.com

TABLE OF CONTENTS

FOREWORD

September 2013 was a month of many changes, during my stay at the Danbury Federal Prison Camp in Danbury, Connecticut. We got word that the Danbury Federal Correctional Institution (the higher security, sister prison that is adjacent to this facility) was being changed to a men's prison. As a result, female prisoners, including Michelle Miles, were transferred from the FCI to the Camp to remain close to their families.

During my first interaction with Michelle we instantly bonded. Her warm inviting spirit, her courage and her tenacity attracted me to her. I couldn't believe after so many years of oppression that she remained positive and sane. As Michelle shared her story, I wept inside because I could personally identify with her pain. The truth is, many of us (prisoners) are trapped in a system that is in "too many respects broken," as recently stated by U.S. Attorney General Eric Holder at the Annual Meeting of the American Bar Association's House of Delegates. Yet, there is no means for us to obtain relief. To the average American citizen we simply represent statistics, because few know our stories or the injustices that we have encountered in the system. I thought my own case was quite extreme, but after hearing Michelle's story I stood dumbfounded, in total disbelief! At that very moment I knew I had to do something. This caused me to step out of my own selfish grief to embrace her fight for freedom.

After sharing my book, "The High Price I Had To Pay," with Michelle, she expressed interest in telling her own story. I immediately connected her with my family at Voices International

Publications and the rest is history! My book was turned into a series that now represents the voices of female offenders in the U.S. prison system. Michelle's story, like my own, exhibits the real-life circumstances of many of us who are serving lengthy sentences in federal prison. She is a modern day voice for those who she refers to as being "buried alive" without a voice.

Collaborating with Michelle on this project has been an honor. Her strength has inspired me to actively engage in the work of prison reform. Michelle made me realize that we need each other to overcome the epidemic of over-incarceration in our nation. Hopefully together we will be a living example to others who are caught in the struggle, inspiring unity and creating change.

For the many who read this book, my prayer is that you will take action! Mass-incarceration is certainly a problem that MUST be addressed. As recently stated by Attorney General Eric Holder, "too many Americans go to too many prisons for too long, and for no truly good law enforcement reason." The problem has been identified, but until it is fixed thousands of prisoners are suffering severe consequences. It is less known that many of the prisoners effected are women who have children that have been left behind. Not only does this epidemic effect prisoners and their families, it also effects our entire country! Tax payers spend hefty dollars to house prisoners serving extremely lengthy sentences. Instead of these prisoners paying their debt back to society in a productive manner that could benefit their communities, tax payers are paying to "warehouse" them.

Michelle's story will enlighten readers to the true faces of women in prison and the underlying circumstances that led to our incarceration. We are not all "monsters or villains." We are people who made mistakes that altered our destinies. Don't throw us away or "warehouse" us! Please share your compassion and mercy and help us to receive the assistance we need to return home to our families as productive members of society. We need your support! Even if it is just a kind word, your help can make a difference! Please visit www.womenoverincarcerated.org to find out how you can lend a helping hand today!

God's Greatest Blessings
Jamila T. Davis

ACKNOWLEDGEMENTS

First and Foremost, I want to thank God. If it had not been for Him, I don't know how I would have made it through the most trying times of my life. His strength was made perfect in my weakness.

To my mother, Joyce Miles, you are such a beautiful, strong black woman. I thank you for all that you have done for me, and thank you for standing by me. You always told me that I deserve better. Forgive me for not listening to your guidance. Please know even though we are apart in this season, I carry you with me in my heart. I love you.

To Lisa Marie Miles, my precious niece, you are the sweetest person I have ever known. Thank you for holding me down all these years, when no one else was around. You have done so much for me. Words can't express my gratitude to you. You are the daughter that I never got a chance to have. Thanks for supporting me both emotionally and financially. From the bottom of my heart, I love you.

To Anthony Shannon, I love you with all my heart. It may have taken you some time to find me, but I am so glad you did! Thank you for loving me and helping me to trust again. You may feel honored, but I feel truly blessed to have you in my life. You have proven to be my lover and my friend. Thanks for sticking through this bid with me.

To Jamila T. Davis, thanks for embracing me with open arms. Real recognizes real! I am so glad we crossed paths. You are truly blessed, and I thank you for being a blessing to me. You inspired me to come out of my box and tell my story. You listened to me, encouraged me and cried with me. And, you helped me with my edits. That meant so much to me. I am truly grateful! A simple thank you really isn't enough. Just know, we are rocking out to the end! Much love to you and your family. I got your back 100%.

INTRODUCTION

"To-date, I have served 16 years of the 30 year sentence that was handed down to me. I feel like I was left here to die, sort of like being buried alive!"

My name is Michelle Miles. I am an African American, 41 year old woman, with no children. It is not that I don't have children by my own choice. My child bearing years were spent behind bars in federal prison.

On September 24, 1997, at the age of 25, I was arrested by the FBI and detained at the Metropolitan Detention Center(MDC) in Brooklyn. In March of 2000, after being convicted at trial, I was sentenced to 360 months (30 years) in federal prison. After I was convicted of conspiracy to traffic heroin and crack cocaine, and one count of distributing crack cocaine, I was labeled by the Feds as a drug "queen pin." I was accused of purchasing drugs, cooking them up, packaging, distributing, hiring workers, setting shifts and collecting money from the sale of these products. At the time of my arrest, I wasn't being watched or investigated. My charges all stem solely on the basis of a government informant who was already serving time in federal custody.

I was sure a jury would never convict me on charges where there was no solid evidence of my guilt, but I was wrong! Not only was I convicted, I was also held accountable for 61.54 kilograms of crack cocaine for a conspiracy that supposedly lasted for 7 years, from 1990-1997. That's how I got so much time!

As a federal inmate, I am left to serve 85% of my time, without recourse. In the Feds their is no parole. With that being said, I have a current out date of 11/27/2023, which leaves me with ten years left to serve in prison. All together, with good time credit, I will be required to serve 26 years of my 30 year sentence. I am serving a sentence that is 30 times greater than the previous maximum drug sentence, before the U.S Sentencing Guidelines were enacted. Prior to the Drug Reform Act of 1986, that was established to combat the "War On Drugs," the longest sentence Congress had ever imposed for possession of any amount of drugs was one year in prison. Even worse, the drastic changes in drug laws have not yielded any success in combating crime. Recent statistics have proven that the rate of crime has not decreased in America. Instead, it has simply increased the amount of people in federal prisons across the country. According to Marc Mauer's book, "Race To Incarcerate," the U.S. prison population has increased from 300,000 to more than 2 million, in less than thirty years, with drug convictions accounting for the majority of the increase. Consequently, families have been separated and many like myself have been "warehoused" in prisons for long periods of time, left without any recourse. I am not saying that we should not have been punished for our crimes, but in many cases "prosecution" has been more like "crucifixion." Is a 30 year sentence for a first-time, 25 year old, female offender considered just?

To-date, I have served 16 years of the 30 year sentence that was handed down to me. I feel like I was left here to die, sort of like being buried alive! I share my story with the hope that someone reading this book will sympathize with my struggles and help me in my fight for freedom. I also share my story with the hope that some young girl reading this book will not make the mistakes that I once made.

This book is not written to make any claims that I am innocent. I fully accept responsibility for the role I played in my crime. I write this book to give readers a glimpse of my background and the circumstances that surrounded my case. I believe I should have been punished for my wrongdoings, but a thirty-year sentence is quite severe! To me, it is totally unjust! Unfortunately, I am not alone. Many women behind bars in federal prison have a similar story as mine. They too are serving similar sentences, some even more severe!

To many I may be forgotten, but I am still alive, and I do have a voice. It is my prayer that my voice will be heard. I hope that you will take the time out to read the details of my case, and ask yourself the questions: (1) Is it fair for a first time, non-violent offender to be sentenced to thirty years in prison? (2) Does America really represent equality and justice for all? You be the judge!

CHAPTER ONE
Born Into The Struggle

"Being born into poverty, I had no clue that there was such a thing as a better life. To me, it was normal to step over urine in the elevator, and pass by dope fiends and drug dealers to get into my apartment."

I was born and raised in the Bedford Stuyvesant section of Brooklyn, New York. I lived in a rundown, three bedroom apartment inside the Marcy Housing Project. From day one, life for me was a struggle. My mother was a single parent who worked hard to raise four children. Although she worked from sun up, to sun down, there were days we barely had any food on the table. During those times, my mother would get creative and stretch the scraps she had to feed us.

Being born into poverty, I had no clue that there was a such thing as a better life. To me, it was normal to step over urine in the elevator, and pass by dope fiends and drug dealers to get into my apartment. Although I probably should have been sad or depressed because of my surroundings, I knew no better. To me, life was grand.

When I was six years old my mother got with my stepfather. At first, it seemed to be good to have a male figure in our home. In the projects it was common to see muggings, stabbings and even shootings occur, so I was glad to have my step-father's protection. Shortly after my step-father moved in with us, back-to-back, my mother had two more children. While my mother worked, my step-father laid around the house and looked after us. Suddenly, his behavior changed drastically. He began to drink a lot and he was often abusive.

One day when I was about 10 years old, I remember sneaking to the bathroom and watching my stepdad through the small crack in the door, which he left slightly open. My stepdad had a belt in his hand. He sat on the toilet and tightly wrapped the belt around his arm. After securing the belt he removed a spoon from his pocket and placed a powdery substance on the spoon. Then, he reached in his pocket and took out a lighter to heat it up. I watched intensely, intrigued by his actions. What shocked me was the very last thing that he did. He tapped his arm and injected the substance into it, using a needle. A few minutes later he fell asleep on the toilet. This became a common routine for him. On one occasion, during his bathroom escape, he didn't wake up. My step-father had turned purple, as his body stood lifeless on the bathroom floor. Immediately upon discovering his body, my brother dialed 911. In attempt to save him, my brother and my uncle placed ice on his groin area and attempted to perform CPR, until the paramedics came. I was frightened that my step-father wouldn't make it. By the grace of God, he was revived. Later that night, my brother told me that my stepdad had OD'd, which stood for over dosed. That's how I found out that he was a heroin addict.

I grew up in a dark place, with no real role models. Everyone that was around me was struggling to survive. Depression had gotten the best of them, so they used alcohol and drugs to numb themselves from the realities of life. My biological father was not in my life at all as a child. He and my mother separated and it seemed like he forgot that he had children. The love and affection that I missed from my dad I tried to get from my step-father. Even though he was an addict, he was the only father figure I knew. Therefore, I let my guard down and embraced him. That is where I went wrong! One day, as a teenager, after one of his binges, my step-father lured my sister and me into his bedroom and he began to fondle my breasts. I asked him to stop, because I knew what he was doing was wrong. But, he didn't. He used his force and robbed me of my innocence. When my mother got home, I told her what happened. She yelled at him, but that was it! I don't know if I was more hurt by what he did or her reaction. At that point, I knew I was alone in this world, left to defend myself.

Shortly after, I ran away from home and moved into my Uncle Rudy's house. He lived in Brooklyn also, not too far from my mother's apartment. Uncle Rudy was my favorite uncle. He showered me with gifts, love and attention. I loved it! I lived with my uncle for about a year, from age 16 to 17 years old. That was the best year of my life! All I had to do was go to school and do chores and I got everything I wanted. For the first time in my life, I had new clothes, shoes, sneakers and coats to wear to school. Everything I always wanted, Uncle Rudy provided for me. More importantly, I had Uncle Rudy's love and affection. I knew he would always care for me and protect me from all harm and danger. That meant everything to me!

My step-father ended up getting very sick and my mother was unable to care for him. At first, I was reluctant to help, but his condition was so bad that I knew it was the right thing to do. Therefore, I moved back in with my mother, and I officially became my step-father's caretaker. His reckless behavior had finally caught up with him. Shortly after I moved back in, he ended up dying from full blown AIDS, which he contracted from intravenous drug usage. I was sad that his life ended so abruptly, but I was relieved to be able to return to my teenage life.

I continued to go to school with hopes that I would one day make it out of the projects. It was my dream to move my entire family to a better place where we no longer had to look over our shoulders. For the next few years life was fine. Then suddenly my world crumbled! My Uncle Rudy, my protector and my provider, passed away. He also was a victim of HIV. This deadly monster ripped through my family with rage. Unlike my stepfather, Uncle Rudy wasn't a drug addict. Unfortunately, fate led him down the same path to death.

For many months I stayed in mourning. Sometimes I would close my eyes and wish I was in heaven with Uncle Rudy. In my mind, death couldn't be worse than the hell I was living in on this earth. During these dark days, I wondered if life would ever deal me a fair hand. At this point, one thing I knew for sure: I was born into the struggle! I had no choice but to find a way to survive.

CHAPTER TWO
Searching For Love

"Inside I always had this inner void. All my life I felt like I was missing something. In my mind, I felt like if I met Prince Charming he would rescue me and my pain would go away. I wanted desperately for someone to hold me, love me and show me affection. I wanted to experience unconditional love, just like I saw on television."

My favorite television show growing up was "The Cosby Show." I was mesmerized with the character "Mr. Huxstable," played by Bill Cosby. I always thought I'd be the luckiest girl in the world if I could be his daughter, which was the character "Rudy." The Cosby Show taught me a lot about life outside the dreary project walls that I was surrounded by. From the show I learned how successful black families lived. Watching the program gave me permission to dream that one day I too could obtain that dream.

For hours, as I stared outside my bedroom window, I would daydream that I was "Rudy." *If I had the life she did, I would have no worries. "Mr. Huxstable" would provide for me, love me and protect me,* I would think to myself. It felt good to day dream, but when reality settled back in, I was left to deal with the truth of my circumstances. I was stuck in a place in life where I didn't want to be, and I was lonely. Inside I always had this inner void. All my life I felt I was missing something. In my mind, I felt like if I met my Prince Charming he would rescue me and my pain would go away. I wanted desperately for someone to hold me, love me and show me affection. I wanted to experience unconditional love, just like I saw on television.

After Uncle Rudy passed away things got substantially worse for me and my entire family. When times got rough, we no longer had Uncle Rudy to fall back on. Almost immediately we suffered the consequences. My mother's sister, my Aunt Dawn, was evicted from her apartment and she and her five children came to live with us in our three bedroom apartment. After she moved in, there were 5 adults and 10 children living in our tiny apartment. To say it was overcrowded was an understatement! I would try to spend as much time as I could outside our apartment to avoid the chaos.

In the summer of 1990, while sitting on the park bench in front of my building, I met this man who began to aggressively pursue me. At first, I was uninterested. I was only 18 years old and the man, whom I later found out was named Stanley Burrell, was 30 years old. He had recently come home from serving a bid in state prison. The girls in my neighborhood looked up to Stan. I guess you could say he was a "top-pick." After his repeated propositions and the death of Uncle Rudy, I eventually gave in. I liked the respect that Stan got in the neighborhood and I felt like he could protect me. Therefore, I decided to give him a chance.

In the beginning of our relationship Stan had no money. We were both poor, but we enjoyed each other's company. When Stan finally came to my mother's house and saw how we were all packed in under one roof, he said he had to do something about my situation. I dismissed it at the time, but by the fiery look in Stan's eyes I should have known he meant business!

Shortly after, I received a phone call from Stan. He advised me to meet him at the apartment of a well known drug addict in our neighborhood. When I arrived at the apartment Stan opened the door and walked me into the kitchen area, which had several people standing around. I was kind of taken back, because I was not accustomed to Stan hanging out with any of these people. As I stared at the kitchen, I noticed their was a substantial amount of a rocky substance laid out on a kitchen plate. I immediately asked Stan what it was? He replied and pointed, "crack cocaine and this over here is heroin." I stood in disbelief. I had watched my step-father shoot up, but I never saw that quantity of drugs up-close. I didn't know whether I should stay or leave. In my mind at the time, heroin was the enemy that was responsible for destroying my family, so I was not receptive at all. I didn't want to show Stan my emotions, so I stood silent and awaited his instructions. Stan pulled me to the side and told me he needed me to help him get back on his feet. He told me he would pay me every week to cook up and bag up the drugs for him, so he could sell them. At first, I rejected his offer, but then he explained the benefits of my participation. Stan said if I worked for him I could make $1100.00 a week. The money he offered enticed me. It was certainly enough for me to take care of myself and my whole family. As he continued to talk about the money, all I could think about was living the life I always dreamed about. Maybe assisting him wouldn't be that bad after all, I thought to myself. It wasn't like I would be actually selling the drugs, right? I let my irrational thinking get the best of me, and I convinced myself that helping Stan with his business was the right thing to do.

Stan taught me all about the drug business. He taught me how to cook the drugs, cut them and bag them up. I instantly caught on and even found ways to stretch Stan's product. He began to call me his "master chef." Almost immediately, the dollars started rolling in. Overnight, I went from rags to riches. Not only did I have enough money to take care of my family, I even had money left over to splurge on myself. In a matter of months I bought everything I always wanted as a child, but couldn't afford. As I stared at myself in the mirror admiring my new clothes and jewelry, I felt good about myself. Money gave me a sense of importance. I was no longer little Michelle. I became Michelle the "get-money chick," which the the guys and girls in my projects respected. And, I loved it! Sad to say, I never thought about any consequences for my actions. All I thought about was gaining as much money as I could get, and finding a way to save as much as I could. I was determined to sustain my newfound lifestyle. I made a vow to myself that I would never be poor again!

As the money rolled in, I fell in love with Stan. He was responsible for changing my life, and I was grateful. To show Stan my appreciation I became his "ride or die" chick. No matter what he needed, I always promised to deliver. In my mind, I owed Stan my life. He became the father figure I never had, because he was older, wiser and more mature. I listened intensely to the advice he gave me, and by following his lead I saw results! My worst fear was Stanley leaving me. If he left, I knew my lifestyle would leave too. Therefore, I tried my best to please him in every way that I could. Stan became the center of my world. In my mind, I finally met my Prince Charming!

CHAPTER THREE
Partners In Crime

"It felt good to be promoted to Stan's partner in the drug operation. The way he presented it, I believed I would be his 'Bonnie,' so I called him my 'Clyde.' I took my pledge seriously. I was even ready to die for the cause. I was all in, and there was no turning back!"

One hot summer day in 1994, Stan entered my bedroom. As we talked, he began to scope out the room. Stan was sort of the jealous type. He didn't want me hanging out with any dudes and he often checked out the scene to make sure I was staying true to him. Stan didn't know he had no worries. The only man I had eyes for was him.

Roaming through my dresser drawer, Stan discovered my stash spot. I had saved up $10,000 from the money he was paying me. I had it hidden safely in the back of my sock drawer, so no one would find it. Stan's curiosity led him to my hiding spot. He immediately asked me how I had gotten the money. I told him every week that he paid me I only spent $100.00 and I saved $1000.00. Stan was surprised and quite impressed. I guess he thought I would blow my money on things I really didn't need. I explained to him it was my goal to get out of the projects and to never be poor again. Immediately, Stan's face lit up with a bright smile. He told me he was proud of me and happy to have me on his team. Stan suggested that I give him the $10,000 and he promised he would double my money for me. He said we would become partners and use the money we made to build a better life for ourselves. To me, his offer was brilliant. If I had Stan's help I knew I could move mountains and achieve all of my goals. Therefore, with no questions asked, I eagerly agreed with a handshake, gave him the money and we officially became partners in crime. It felt good to be promoted to Stan's partner in the drug operation. The way he presented it, I believed I would be his "Bonnie," so I called him my "Clyde." I took my pledge seriously. I was even ready to die for the cause. I was all in, and there was no turning back!

My excitement was short lived. Although Stan said we were partners, I felt more like his girl friend with a few extra perks. Prior to me joining in, Stan had already had his operation set up. His three homeboys, David Moore aka Boom, Shannon Carr aka Boo-Boo and Howard Migette aka How-Bow, were the main players who ran the day-to-day operations. They set the shifts and hired the workers. Shannon was like the watchdog. He made sure the workers didn't steal any money. The boys protected Stan from outsiders. They ran the street affairs, but Stan was the real boss. All moves that were to be executed had to be run by Stan first for approval. Stan kept things in order and he kept the money flowing in, so his homeboys followed his lead.

After I became a "partner," Stan instructed his team to deliver the money collected from the workers to me. By that time, he had a large part of the projects on lock. Stan controlled the drug trade on Nostrand Avenue, between Myrtle Avenue and Park Avenue. This was the main block for drug traffic in the neighborhood. In a short period of time, after my investment, Stan became the man in the hood. And, he wanted everyone to know it!

Stan got rid of his white Cutlass Sierra, which had a blue rag top, and he bought a brand new Cherokee Jeep. He decked out his car with nice rims and a stereo system that was out of this world! You could literally hear Stan's jeep blocks before he actually approached. When Stan pulled his jeep up to the projects, he immediately became a "hood legend." It seemed like everywhere I went people were bragging about Stan and his new ride. Shortly after, they gave Stan the nick name "Stan-The Man"

Overnight Stan changed before my eyes, and not just in appearance. Stan was really feeling himself. He became cocky and self-centered. Every other day Stan was buying more and more things. He had more jewelry than he knew what to do with. As time went on, and the money kept rolling in, Stan bought cars like he was buying candy. Stan bought an Infiniti Q45, a Mercedes Benz, an Acura Legend and a BMW, all back-to-back. Stan even helped his homeboys buy cars too. Boom drove a white Cherokee Jeep, just like Stan's red one. And, Boo-Boo drove a Ford Expedition, Eddie Bauer edition. Although I was suppose to be a partner, I wasn't a part of Stan's car shopping sprees. It seemed like he wanted me carless, so I would be dependent on him. After I complained, because I felt like I was being left out, Stan bought me a gold Honda Accord with a Brown rag top. I believe he bought it to shut me up. My car was not brand new like the boys cars and his. But, I was happy to be driving, so I didn't complain.

For Stan's 35th Birthday, he rented out a bar in my neighborhood, which was the official hang out spot. Sean "Jay-Z" Carter, who grew up in the building right next to mine, performed. This was before his "Reasonable Doubt" album was released. I couldn't believe how crazy the girls were going over Sean. To me, Sean was like a big brother because we knew each other for so many years. Therefore, it was hard to envision him as a rap star, at first. But that quickly changed! As Sean rapped, the crowd went wild and Moet was passed around like it was water. Sean's stage presence commanded respect, causing the whole hood to have to recognize him by his stage name Jay-Z. Stan's celebration was fit for a king! Stan's boys, Jay-Z and Jay-Z's best friend, Ty-Ty, showed Stan mad love that night. From the looks of things the Marcy boys were all headed out of the projects onto the road of success. It was like watching a "rags-to-riches" story unfold right in front of my eyes! It was certainly an event to remember!

By July of 1995, Stan's operation was thriving. Stan was officially the man in our area. He gained his respect, but at the same time he also attracted the envy of other drug dealers in our neighborhood. A few even attempted to take Stan's life, but Stan always managed to escape. At this point, my role in the operation was to cook up the drugs, bag them up and give them to Boo-Boo, How-Bow and Boom to distribute. In exchange for the packages, the boys would drop me the money made from the sales on the block. Every dollar I collected went straight to Stan. As time went on, I begin to feel like I was being used. Once Stanley started attracting a lot of attention to himself, he began to cheat on me with several different women. Stanley had one child which I knew about, which was his daughter Tynaisha. His daughter's mother was a girl named Monique, who lived near our projects. She was the only girl Stan ever mentioned. Prior to Stan blowing up, he never seemed to pay much attention to women. After he started getting money, things changed! The girls in the neighborhood continuously tried to tip me off to Stan's cheating, but I didn't want to believe them. In my mind, I pictured Stan only being true to me. I thought I was his "Bonnie," because our pledge was suppose to be for life. Unfortunately, it was one-sided. I played my part, but he left me hanging.

One day while sitting on the project bench in front of my building a light skinned girl rolled a stroller up to me. From the pictures I had seen of her, I knew she was Stan's daughter's mother, Monique. She had a new born baby in the the stroller. Curiosity got the best of me, so I asked her to see her baby. To my surprise the new born looked just like Stan! Inside I wanted to die. I felt like such a fool! I asked Monique the baby's name and she replied "Stanley Jr." Fortunately, I didn't pass out right there on the spot. I knew I couldn't let this girl see me sweat, so I did my best to keep my composure.

That night it took everything in me not to act a fool. I wanted to beat the brakes off of Monique, but I realized it was not her fault. Stan was the true culprit. I could no longer pretend not to see. I was forced to wake up to the truth! As I cringed within my soul, I wanted Stan to feel the same pain I was experiencing. I made up in my mind that I had to finally let Stan go, so I put forth my best effort to execute my mission. Later that evening when I finally saw Stan, he lied to my face and told me the baby was not his. I wanted to believe him, but the newborn's features resembled Stan to the letter. I didn't have the courage or the strength to walk away, so I went against my better judgment and I stayed. As a result, my life was miserable.

After this event, different girls kept popping up. I couldn't stand the hurt and betrayal that I felt, so I started lashing out. I began to fight Stan and every girl who claimed she was with him. I didn't care who was around or how my behavior appeared. As a result, people in our projects thought I was losing my mind. Others thought I was turning into a beast. Jay-Z nick named me "Tyson" after he witnessed me knocking a few girls out over Stan. It was clear at this point I had lost control! Looking in the mirror, I no longer liked the reflection I saw. Inside I felt like I was less than I was suppose to be. In my mind, if I had possessed the complete package Stan would not have cheated on me. As my image shattered in my mind, I lost my self-esteem. I wasn't crazy as many had accused me of being. The truth was that I was crazy in love. I loved someone unconditionally who clearly did not have the same feelings about me. The problem was, I was too weak to let him go. He had been my protector and my provider for so many years, that I felt I could not live without him. Even when I finally built up the strength to walk away, I was quickly lured back. Stan had such a way with words. He knew just how to wheel me back in. Regardless of how he treated me, I was determined to hold Stan down to the fullest, and he knew it.

As time went by, things for me got worse. After my first couple of attempts to walk away from our relationship, Stan tried his best to tighten the reins on me. He believed the way to control me was to limit the money that I had access to. Therefore, Stan no longer paid me on a regular basis. I would get money from time to time, only if I asked. And, the money I did get, Stan would try his best to manage what I did with it. Sometimes if I was lucky he would buy me things, but that was only if I followed his rules. And, remember the $10,000 I invested to be a partner in his operation, I never got a dime of that money back. At the time I couldn't see it, but I was certainly being played, just like a fiddle.

My mother observed my reckless lifestyle and she hated it, even though I was able to help my family out financially. At times, my lifestyle appeared to improve, but I was still not happy. I escaped the imprisonment of poverty only to be locked into another prison within my soul. I was an inmate and Stan played the role of a prison guard. I could come out of my cell, only if he let me. Believing I couldn't survive without him, I held on to the dream that things would eventually get better. I hoped to one day be Stan's wife, have his kids and live behind a white picket fence in the suburbs. That never happened!

In the end, the partnership I thought we had turned out to be a curse. I became a slave to the person I loved most, and he became my master!

CHAPTER FOUR
The Busts

"Within seconds, a car pulled up and several agents jumped out! Once again, I heard the words that became common to hear, "You are under arrest." As I read the letters "F.B.I." on the officers' jackets, I knew for sure this time my fate would never be the same. I was doomed!"

In early 1995, Stan's brother, Brian Burrell aka Bee-Wop, came home from serving a 5 year bid in state prison. Directly following his release, Bee-Wop joined Stan's drug operation. Because he was Stan's brother, he was immediately promoted to a higher rank than the other key players in the operation. This automatically bred jealousy and caused internal friction within the organization. Adding fuel to the fire, Stan made me his Comptroller. I controlled the handling of the proceeds made. All money collected had to be brought to me before anyone got paid. It was my job to count the money and turn it over to Stan. During my collections, several times the money came up short. The boys would tell me the stacks of money that they handed me were one amount, but when I counted them, they were not! This caused further problems, because I would often confront the boys and we got into heated debates. It was my belief that the boys were intentionally stealing from Stan and setting up their own business on the side. I tried to tip Stan off to the scheme, but he wouldn't take heed. Stan trusted his boys, so you couldn't tell him anything when it came to them.

Stan's homeboys meant everything to him. He would buy them all kinds of things, including cars and jewelry. The boys all grew up together in the projects, so they were more like brothers than friends. I often felt left out. In my mind, I thought Stan love his friends more than he loved me. For example, when I would check his boys about the money being short, and they told Stan, he would yell at me for arguing with them. Eventually, I got fed up with what was going on, so I quit my position in the organization. I figured I'd be better off just playing the role of Stan's girlfriend. After I backed out my position, Stan's operation swiftly began to go down hill. Once I was out of the picture, at every chance they could get, his team started rampantly stealing money. I didn't care at that point. I figured that was Stan's problem and he'd finally put them in their place.

After I made my exit, things seemed to get better with me and Stan. I no longer had to deal with the stress of the business, and he still provided for me. I was good for a minute, or at least I thought I was. I finally began to settle down and live a normal life.

In May of 1995, I attended a baby shower at my mother's apartment. There was a large turn out for the function, so her tiny apartment was packed from wall-to-wall. During the baby shower I had to use the bathroom, and my mother's bathroom was occupied. Therefore, I decided to go downstairs to Ms. Angela, my niece's grandmother's house. Ms. Angela, like many of the residents who lived in the projects, was a drug addict. On occasions she did favors for Stan and his boys. She would allow them to cook up and store drugs in her apartment for drugs or money.

After I used Ms. Angela's bathroom, I was headed out the door, on my way back upstairs. Before I could reach the front door of her apartment, I walked straight into a police officer. The officer had Mr. Willie, Ms. Angela's husband, in handcuffs, directly in front of the apartment, and he was entering the premises to conduct a search. "Put your hands up, you are under arrest," another officer yelled as a team of officers entered the apartment. I stood in disbelief. I couldn't believe what was happening!

The officers made me stand up against the wall as they began to search Ms. Angela's house. A few minutes after they had entered, they discovered a drug stash in the apartment. Consequently, Ms. Angela, Mr. Willie and myself were hauled off to the local police station, where we were detained and later sent to central booking. After seeing a magistrate judge, we were all housed at Riker's Island until our arraignment. As I laid on a flimsy mattress inside my prison cell, tears began to stream down my face. I was nervous and frightened. I had no clue what was going to happen next! For the first time, I thought about the consequences for the reckless lifestyle I was living, and I broke down and cried. Although the drugs in the apartment had nothing to do with me, I felt like karma was catching up to me and I had no place to hide. I was hit! Right in front of my eyes, my world came crashing down!

Even though we were all charged with 5 counts, to my surprise, when I went in front of the judge he released me on a R.O.R., so I didn't even have to post any bail. As I walked out the doors of the court room as a free woman, I sighed in relief. I was scared straight! I wanted no parts of anybody's drug business or illegal dealings. I made a vow to God that day that I would straighten out my life and do the right thing, and I tried my best to keep my promise. Following my arrest, I enrolled back in school, and I sought God daily to give me the strength I needed to stay on the right path in life.

My state case went on for two years. The prosecutor wanted me to take a plea. I felt like I shouldn't because I had nothing to do with the drugs, although I later found out that the drugs belonged to Stan. After going back and forth in negotiations, and exceeding the time to settle the case, trial was set. By this time, Mr. Willie had died and Ms. Angie turned state. I was shocked to learn that my long term family friend was scheduled to testify against me. But, I proceeded to trial with confidence believing the truth would prevail and justice would be rendered on my behalf.

In February of 1997, I entered the tiny court room, in the Brooklyn Superior Court House, dressed professionally in a dark pant suit, as instructed by my attorney. I was nervous as the reality of what was happening finally settled in. The jury was picked and Ms. Angie took the stand. It was clear by her testimony that I wasn't the only one who was nervous. Ms. Angie rocked back and forth on the stand, like a crazy woman, and she mumbled through her response. In the middle of her testimony, she even got down from the stand, grabbed her purse and popped pills. She did this several times, until the judge finally scolded her. At times during questioning, she even became belligerent. It became quite amusing to some of the jurors who began to laugh as they watched her performance. When asked who did the drugs belong to, she said they were mine, but she stuttered answering questions about her alleged interactions with me. Thank God the jury didn't buy her testimony. After a three week trial, which ended with me testifying in my defense, I was acquitted on all charges. The verdict was rendered just three days before my 25th birthday.

I sighed in relief, happy that this long ordeal was finally over. Tears of joy rolled down my eyes, as the judge announced that the case was dismissed. I thanked God for the victory, believing I was done with my past and could finally live a law-biding life, absent of drama. Before I could exit the courtroom, to my surprise, I was re-arrested on the spot and escorted into a courtroom adjacent to the one I had just left. I just couldn't catch a break!

The case they were trying to charge me with stemmed from a raid that happened back in 1996. My mother, my two brothers, my sister, my cousin and my uncle were all arrested in my mother's apartment. My mother's house was raided and the police found drugs that belonged to my younger brother, who also sold drugs. Although I wasn't present in the apartment during the raid, my acquittal prompted the police to charge me with possession. I guess in their minds they had to get me with something.

I stood in front of another judge, dumb founded. It was like I had become an involuntary actress in a horror movie. I couldn't believe what was happening. It was clearly not fair! Thank God this judge agreed that what I was experiencing was malicious prosecution. He declared that the police did not have enough evidence to charge me and he dismissed the case on the spot. I was finally a free woman, with no strings attached. I swiftly gathered my belongings and exited the court house as quickly as I could. I refused to look back! I didn't want any parts of the judicial system. My short stint with the law taught me that the police didn't play fair. If they wanted you, they would go to extremes to lock you down, at any cost!

After the trial my life was finally back on track. I was grateful for my second chance to get things right. Stan and I became distant. I still dealt with him, but I made it my business to stay far away from his business affairs. I had learned my lesson!

On September 24, 1997, late in the evening, just 7 months after my acquittal, I met Stan at his apartment. We finally decided to have a heart-to-heart talk. We talked for hours and reminisced about old times. It felt good to finally discuss how I felt about everything that had happened and how I felt he mistreated me. We made amends and I left his apartment. I exited Stan's building feeling good about finally confronting my fears and discussing my true feelings. As I got close to the corner, I heard a female voice shout my name. When I turned around a lady and a man, who were both neatly dressed, approached me and instructed me to freeze. Within seconds, a car pulled up and several federal agents jumped out! Once again I heard the words which became common to hear, "You are under arrest." As I read the letters "F.B.I." on the officers' jackets, I knew for sure this time my fate would never be the same. I was doomed!

Tears flowed uncontrollably as I left the projects handcuffed in the back of the police car. I knew in my heart this was going to be the last time I'd see my neighborhood in a very long time. I had no clue what was up ahead, but I knew it wasn't good! This time I made it on to the radar of the big boys. I was busted by the FEDS!

CHAPTER FIVE
The Discovery

"For months I was in the dark about how my federal charge came about. A few months after I was arrested, on an attorney visit, the puzzle finally came together. Over and over, I read the discovery documents in disbelief. It had to be a mistake, I thought. But what was in black and white could not be denied. I was betrayed!"

On September 24, 1997, after I was arrested, I was taken to the Federal Building at 26 Federal Plaza to be processed. This time I was not alone. The FEDS also arrested Stan. As we both entered the building handcuffed, standing side-by-side, he told me we had no worries because they didn't have anything on us.

I was shaken to the core! In a matter of months I had more interactions with the law than some seasoned criminals have in a lifetime! And, this time, I graduated from the State to the FEDS. *What horrible luck?*, I thought to myself. I could tell by the glare in the lead agent's eyes things were going to be difficult. My notion was quickly confirmed. When Stan and I went before the judge, he honored the prosecutor's request. The prosecutor argued that Stan and I were both flight risks. With no money and no place to go, where could I possibly run to? Within moments, the judge banged his gavel and declared,

"Bail denied," and my escapade through the U.S. judicial system officially began. I was trapped!

Escorted by U.S. Marshall agents, I landed in Manhattan, New York, at the Metropolitan Correctional Center (MCC), where I sat for several months waiting for my attorney to help me get to the bottom of things. I was charged with one count of conspiracy to sell crack cocaine, without any drugs being confiscated from me or Stan. I didn't understand how that was possible in America. I held tightly to Stan's words, "We have nothing to worry about. They have nothing on us." I prayed daily that what he said was the truth. For months I was in the dark about how my federal charge came about. A few months after I was arrested, on an attorney visit, the puzzle finally came together. Over and over, I read the discovery documents in disbelief. It had to be a mistake, I thought. But what was in black and white could not be denied. I was betrayed!

On February 8, 1995, Andre Thomas aka Dre, one of Stan's associates whom we grew up with in the projects, was pulled over by the Maryland State troopers. His vehicle was searched and the troopers discovered 300 grams of crack cocaine. Along with the drugs the troopers also found drug paraphernalia, i.e. baggies, a scale, razor blades, etc.

According to the discovery documents, when the troopers questioned Dre almost immediately he told them that the drugs belonged to Michelle Banks. He said he received written instructions to deliver the drugs to someone in North Carolina. Although my legal name is Michelle Miles, my mother's maiden name is Banks. In my neighborhood, the Banks family name is well known. Even though there was never any note found during the search, the troopers found Dre's statement credible and turned his case over to the FBI.

Upon being interviewed by the FBI, Dre gave the same story, but he added that this was his second trip. He stated on the first trip he made it successfully to his destination, with no problems. He further stated that Michelle Banks, referring to me, had heard he had fallen on hard times and I wanted to help him out. His statement was the furthest thing from the truth! I had never been out of state in my life, nor did I know anyone who lived in North Carolina! I had no knowledge what Dre was doing, and I hadn't even had any real contact with him since we were little. His story was totally made up! My only dealings with drugs was through Stan's organization. I handled the collection of money, and upon Stan's instructions, I gave packages to the key players in his operation. Dre was certainly not part of Stan's operation. And to my knowledge, Stan never did any drug business with him either. It was hard for me to grasp the fact that Dre had made up such a huge lie. Worse than that, the FEDS accepted his statement as factual and Dre didn't even know my correct last name. In my mind, this was all crazy!

As I continued to read the discovery documents, I got even more furious! After Dre got arrested, from behind bars, he began to cooperate with the FEDS. Dre lured his girlfriend into his plan to set up Stan and his team with the FEDS. According to the discovery, Dre's girlfriend set up a drug deal with Shannon Carr aka Boo-Boo. Boo-Boo was a key player in Stan's operation, and he was also Stan's best friend. Boo-Boo was arrested on the spot and detained by the FEDS. Just like Dre, Boo-Boo began to cooperate with the FEDS almost immediately. He collaborated the story that I was the lead person in the operation. And, he gave the FEDS a statement on me, but he didn't mention Stan's name at all. Boo-Boo was like family to me. He always talked about how loyal he was and how much of a stand up dude he was. Therefore, none of what I was reading made any kind of sense, at the time. I couldn't believe what he had done to me!

I stood in disbelief as I read the documents, over and over. The boys were the ones who made all the money, drove the latest cars and rocked endless amounts of designer clothes. And, they made it out to the FEDS that they were all working for me. Really? I was outraged! My attorney handed me a tissue to wipe my tears, and he passed me a superseding indictment. The new indictment added the drugs confiscated from Andre Thomas to me. With this new information on record, I was charged with an additional count of possession for the drugs they caught Dre with.

As I returned to my cell, I began to question whether or not I wanted to stay alive. My insides felt like they were ripped apart. I felt so hurt, belittled and betrayed. I couldn't believe I was facing such serious charges, which were all based on the lies from informants who made statements to get their own charges reduced. I couldn't believe it was legal in America to be charged with a crime simply based on the statement of a convicted felon, without any real evidence to back up their statement. It shouldn't be legal, but that is what happened to me!

After I explained my story to my attorney, he told me that I should not plead guilty to the charges. He advised me that I was looking at a sentence of approximately 10 years in prison, and my best bet was to take the case to trial. Stan also advised me to follow the attorney's advice. Based on their recommendation, I figured I had nothing to lose, so I followed my attorney's lead. Once again, a jury would be left to decide my fate.

CHAPTER SIX
The Trial

"The government's entire case was based on the testimony of informants who were looking to reduce their own charges, and a police officer who testified about a case that I was ultimately acquitted of. In my eyes, their evidence was weak. The prosecutor certainly couldn't prove that I was guilty beyond reasonable doubt. Therefore, I was good, I thought."

On a cold morning in February of 1999 my trial officially began. With Stan's help, I had retained attorney George Sheinberg to represent me. Stan said he was one of the best. Prior to trial, I got cold feet. After hearing the girls that I was locked up with talk about how harsh the FEDS were with people who lost trial, I considered for the first time taking a plea. When I asked Mr. Sheinberg to assist me, he advised me if I was to take a plea he would no longer represent me. I didn't want to lose his assistance, so I got the guts to move ahead and trial proceeded.

I went to trial along with Stan, his brother, Brian Burrell and my youngest brother Darryl Banks. We were all charged with one count of conspiracy. I was also charged with one count of possession from Andre Thomas' arrest. Stan was additionally charged with one count of Continuing Criminal Enterprise (CCE). And, my brother was additionally charged with possession, which resulted from the drugs that were found in my mother's house during the raid back in 1996. Although my brother's drugs had nothing whatsoever to do with me or Stan's operation, the FEDS linked him to me simply because of his relationship to me.

Each morning, I was taken from MCC Detention Center to the Brooklyn Federal Courthouse for trial. I was dressed out of my prison clothes, and I changed into street clothes each day of the trial. The jurors were not allowed to see me in my prison attire or in handcuffs. After being locked up for 17 months, it felt good to feel like a free woman in the courtroom.

From left to right, my attorney and I sat directly next to Stan and his attorney, followed by Bryan and his attorney, and my brother and his attorney. The Assistant District Attorney sat on the opposite side. The court was packed with spectators, friends and family, when jury selection began. Things started off smooth, until the prosecutor presented their witnesses.

First up was federal informant Ada Vega. She was a young girl who also lived in Marcy Housing Projects. Ada was arrested by the FBI in 1997 on drug charges. While detained at the Metropolitan Detention Center (MDC) in Brooklyn, there was a routine shakedown and Ada was found in possession of a cigarette box that contained marijuana and cocaine. Her urine was tested immediately following, and she tested positive for both substances. At the time, Ada was already facing a 10 year sentence for the drug charge she was being detained on. With the drugs confiscated at MDC, which would result in a new charge, she faced a substantial increase in her sentence. In exchange for a more lenient sentence, Vega testified against me.

During the trial, Ada testified that I was Stanley's girlfriend. She told the jurors that I carried a gun, and I cooked up drugs for Stan's operation. I knew of Ada from our neighborhood, but I had very little contact with her. She was not a friend nor a close associate who would have access to my personal dealings. Based on Ada's testimony, the government sought to charge me with possession of a gun that was never found, and for drugs never seized in my case. Ada's testimony resulted in her serving only two years in federal prison, and she was never charged for the drugs confiscated from her at MDC. The day she testified against me, she walked out of the court room as a free woman.

Next up was Andre Thomas aka Dre. On February 8, 1995, after being pulled over by the Maryland State Troopers, Andre was arrested when 300 grams of crack cocaine was confiscated from a shoe box, which also contained drug paraphernalia i.e., baggies, razor blades, a scale, etc, was discovered in his vehicle.

Andre testified that he was delivering the drugs for me with written instructions on where to drop them off in North Carolina, and he stated I had rented the car he was driving. During cross-examination, my attorney was able to bring out the fact that no written letter was found during the search of the car, and there was no proof that I had ever rented a car on his behalf.

Andre was facing 10 years in federal prison due to his charges. In exchange for his testimony he received a 49 month sentence in prison. Like Ada Vega, after testifying against me, Andre walked out of the courtroom a free man.

The last person who testified against me was Officer Donavan, the officer who arrested me during the raid at Ms. Angela's house back in 1995. I felt like bringing him into my trial was double jeopardy, because I was already acquitted of the charges that Officer Donovan testified about. The judge allowed him to introduce the evidence to the jury that I was charged with 5 counts in the State case, but as a court stipulation, he was not allowed to tell the jury I was acquitted on all charges. Consequently, Officer Donavan's testimony left the jury to draw their own conclusions as to what happened with the first case, which was automatically damaging to my defense.

Shannon Carr aka Boo-Boo never showed up to testify against me in court, but through a court stipulation, his statement was read into the record. In sum, the evidence that the FEDS presented against me was the testimony of Ada Vega, Andre Thomas and Officer Donavan, and a statement by Shannon Carr was read into the record. There were no drugs or guns confiscated from me presented as exhibits. The government's entire case was based on the testimony of informants who were looking to reduce their own charges, and a police officer who testified about a case that I was ultimately acquitted of. In my eyes, their evidence was weak. The prosecutor certainly couldn't prove that I was guilty beyond reasonable doubt. Therefore, I was good, I thought.

During the trial, no informants testified against Stan or his brother, Brian. The only evidence the FEDS had against them was the testimony of the Marcy Housing Police and the 79th Precent police. Both testified that from 1990-1997 many people who were arrested mentioned Stan and his brother's names as their suppliers. Based on this hearsay, Stan was charged with a Continued Criminal Enterprise (CCE) and his brother was charged with Conspiracy.

Against my brother, Darryl Banks, informant Future Callwood testified on the government's behalf. Although Future did in fact know my brother, he had no connection whatsoever to me or Stan. That didn't stop him from lying on the stand. Future testified that my brother sold drugs as a member of Stan's organization, which was a complete lie!

After a three week trial, the jury deliberated for several hours before returning a guilty verdict. Despite the limited evidence that was presented against us, the jury found all of us guilty on all charges. I was distraught as the reality of the tough sentence I faced had finally sunken in. Court was adjourned and a sentencing date was set. I could no longer avoid the wrath of what was ahead. I was devastated!

After I lost the trial, my attorney told me I was looking at a life sentence in prison for my conviction. I was dumbfounded! Never in our discussions had he said life in prison was even a possibility! He told me I faced 10 years in prison. Had I known that I would face life if I lost trial, I would have never proceeded with the trial. I would have taken a plea to save myself. For many nights after my attorney's visit, I lost sleep thinking about my sentencing. I couldn't imagine at 27 years old, spending the rest of my life in prison. I knew my participation in Stan's organization was wrong, but I certainly didn't believe that it warranted a life sentence in prison.

On March 24, 2000, I entered the chambers of Honorable Eugene H. Nickerson as a nervous wreck. By sentencing time, I was skin and bones. I lost several pounds because I lacked the desire to eat. Truthfully, I wished I was dead. The time I faced was too much for me to handle.

My attorney argued that I had no criminal record and I was facing an inordinate amount of time in prison. He said he couldn't comprehend that a life sentence would fit the punishment for my crime. My judge seemed to agree with him. He asked my attorney for help in justifying a reduced sentence.

My sentence was calculated based on the 2000 version of the U.S. Sentencing Guidelines. The guidelines, at the time, dictated what range a federal judge was mandated to sentencing a defendant by. I was a level 44, category 1, based on the government's drug calculation that Stan's organization from 1990-1997 had sold over 61 kilos. At the time, my attorney could have argued that I didn't join the conspiracy until 1993 and I withdrew prior to the operation's collapse, but he failed to mitigate the drug calculation. Fortunately, my judge decided to reduce my guideline calculation by two levels. He stated that he believed I was beholden to Stan because I was his girlfriend, and Stan was "the leader of the band." I was grateful that the judge had some compassion, but I was still not prepared from what was to come. After a short argument presented by my lawyer and the prosecutor, Judge Nickerson sentenced me to 360 months in federal prison, which equates to 30 years.

Words can't describe my feelings at that moment in court. In my mind, I had no reason to live. I didn't know how I would make it through this ordeal. It was only the grace of God that kept me!

CHAPTER SEVEN
Life In Prison

"Since my incarceration, I have actively participated in the educational programs and the apprenticeships that the BOP offers. I have made a choice to be productive during my prison stay. I wanted to gain as many skills as I could, so I would be marketable upon my release."

After I was sentenced on March 24, 2000, my boyfriend Stanley Burrell was sentenced to Life in federal prison, without the possibility of parole. His brother, Brian Burrell received the same Life sentence. And, my younger brother, Darryl Banks, was sentenced to 15 years in prison. As federal inmates we are all required to serve 85% of our time, with good time credit. In 1984 parole was abolished for federal prisoners. Therefore, without a sentence reduction or a pardon, I will not be released from prison until 10 years from now, November of 2023.

On June 9, 2000, I was committed to the Federal Correctional Institution in Tallahassee, Florida. I had no clue how I ended up over 1,000 miles away from my family in Brooklyn, New York. Prison life was a big adjustment for me. I quickly had to get acclimated to my new life, which included a new job in food service, which paid me only 12 cents an hour. At first, I found it very rough to take care of myself from the wages that I was receiving. Nothing in prison is free except for three meals each day, our uniforms and toilet paper. All of our other toiletries and clothing items have to be purchased. It is almost impossible to obtain essential items a prisoner needs, without outside help. My mother and my niece do what they can to support me financially, but realistically I have had to rely mostly on the money I earn at my prison job.

Almost immediately, when I was locked behind prison doors, I noticed I was not alone in my circumstances. Several women I met, especially African Americans, were serving lengthy time for drug sentences. Some were even serving life sentences for non-violent drug crimes. This was ludicrous to me! I had to mentally accept the hand that I was dealt, and make the best of it. Doing so was not easy!

I stayed in Tallahassee for approximately 19 months. At the time, the Bureau Of Prisons (BOP) had a contract to house inmates with the State of West Virginia. I was selected to be transferred to Fluvanna State Prison. I stayed there until September 12, 2002, then I was shipped to Danbury Federal Correctional Institution.

Since my incarceration, I have actively participated in the educational programs and the apprenticeships that the BOP offered. I have made a choice to be productive during my prison stay. I wanted to learn as many skills as I could, so I would be marketable upon my release. While incarcerated, I have earned my high school diploma and completed the BOP's Culinary Arts program. I graduated from the program with honors and became a Culinary Arts tutor. For the last 9 years, I've worked at UNICOR, which is a government work program where inmates prepare parts for the U.S. military. At UNICOR, I have served as an Administrative Assistant, production Clerk and Payroll/ Timekeeping Clerk. During my incarceration, I have also completed three apprenticeship programs from the United States

Department of Labor, which include Cook Apprenticeship, 2009 (6000 hrs), Office Manager/Administrative Services- 2012 (4000 hrs) and Material Coordinator- 2013 (4000 hrs). Additionally, I enrolled in Ashworth College to earn my Associates in Psychology. Participating in the educational programs has kept me busy and has also inspired me to proactively fight for my freedom.

I was elated in 2007 when Congress first changed the drug sentencing laws, and introduced the Fair Sentencing Act of 2007. By this point, I had already lost my direct appeal and had exhausted all of my post conviction relief options. Therefore, I was excited to gain another open door to be able to fight for my freedom.

After continuously petitioning the court for counsel to represent me in the filing of my motion, based on the new law, I was finally appointed counsel. On April 3, 2009, my attorney filed a 3582 motion for a sentence modification pursuant to the Fair Sentencing Act of 2007. I waited patiently for several years to gain a response back from the District Court where I was sentenced. As I waited, I watched numerous offenders, who served time with me, gain immediate releases based on the new law, so I remained hopeful that my chance at freedom was near.

On April 2, 2012, after Congress passed another law to further reduce drug sentences, my attorney filed an additional 3582 motion, pursuant to the Fair Sentencing Act of 2010. After waiting for an answer for over three years on the first motion, in July of 2012, I received a letter informing me that I was denied a reduction on both motions. Once again, I was devastated! In my heart I felt like I just couldn't catch a break. Congress made their intent clear to provide fairer sentences for drug offenders who were sentenced under the harsh laws incited by the "War on Drugs," yet some of us were not privileged to receive any of these reductions. According to the courts, because the drug quantity in my case was 61.54 kilograms, I did not qualify for any relief through the new laws. I was greatly disappointed, because this quantity should have been disputed by my lawyer prior to my sentencing in 2000. With no drugs confiscated from me, and only 300 grams confiscated from Andre Thomas, I didn't feel I should have been held responsible for an estimated 61.54 kilograms, especially without any proof. Unfortunately, my beliefs are not considered in the U.S. judicial system. Drug sentences are strictly imposed based on the law. When you are charged with Conspiracy, the word of an informant is enough to hold you accountable for the drug quantity that the informant attests that you handled.

To date, I have served 16 years in federal prison. At 41 years old, I have missed out on my child bearing years. Since my incarceration my mother has been ill, which makes it difficult for her to come visit me. I haven't seen her face-to-face since 2006. Most recently, on January 23, 2013, my father, Michael Bryant, passed away. Because of my charges, and the time left on my sentence, I was unable to attend his funeral. Every time I phone home, I pray that everything is alright. I desperately wish I could be home to care for my ailing mother who needs me.

Despite my hardships, I haven't given up hope. I have faith that God will deliver me and give me a second opportunity at life in the very near future. Upon my release, it is my goal to talk to young people across the country. I want to warn them about the detriments of making poor choices. If someone I respected and I could relate to, would have warned me about the severe consequences I faced, I would not have chosen to take the path that I did.

I want to make it clear that I fully accept responsibility for my criminal behavior. I definitely made the choice to participate in criminal activities, which was nobody's fault but my own. I deserved to be punished for my participation, but I argue that the sentence I received was extremely harsh. This book was not written to play the victim role or to declare my innocence. Instead, it was written to enlighten others to my life circumstances and the obstacles I faced in the U.S. judicial system. For over 16 years, I have been buried alive in the system. To many, my voice has been forgotten, yet I am still alive. I not only represent myself, I represent the many other woman who are housed behind bars, with no way out. We certainly need your help! Please, urge our law makers to look into the lengthy sentences of drug offenders and give us a second chance at life. Your compassion and mercy has the ability to set us free!

AFTERWORD

I pray that after reading my book you have been further enlightened about the lives of women in federal prison and the dilemmas that drug offenders face in the U.S. judicial system.

To date, my 16 years of incarceration has cost tax payers approximately $640,000 to house me in federal prison. I still have 10 years left to serve on my 30 year sentence, which will cost tax payers approximately $400,000 more. In total, my incarceration will cost in excess of one million dollars!

I have taken every program the BOP offers, and I have completed numerous apprenticeships. Therefore, there is nothing more left that I can do behind bars to further serve rehabilitative purposes, yet I still have ten years left to serve on my sentence. Most recently, Attorney General Eric Holder has stated that many prisoners are "warehoused" in prisons across the country. I am a real-life example of one of the people that he refers to. I am trapped inside the U.S. justice system!

After serving such a significant amount of time in prison, I have certainly learned my lesson. My greatest hope is to regain my freedom and be afforded the opportunity to go back into the community to repay my debt to society. I wish to give my service to others. It is my desire to educate youth to the detriment of poor choices. I would like to speak to young girls in particular and introduce them to alternatives to crime and help them to combat low self-esteem. My hope is that by sharing my story, they won't make the same mistakes that I did.

It is my request that you lend me your hand to help me regain my freedom. Your support can make a difference! If federal parole is reinstated it would open the prison doors for many women, such as myself, who are trapped behind bars. Please support this cause by going to www.womenoverincarcerated.org, and sign the online petition addressed to Congress requesting them to reinstate parole. If parole is reinstated, It would provide an outside independent source to evaluate our individual cases and determine our readiness to reenter society. Without parole, many of us are left to serve very lengthy sentences, without any recourse. Therefore, we need your help!

If you are interested in giving me feedback about my story, or words of encouragement. You can write me directly at the address below:

Michelle Miles #48851-053
Danbury Federal Prison Camp
33 1/2 Pembroke Rd.
Danbury, CT 06811

You are important to me. Therefore, I would love to hear from you! Thanks for taking the time to read this book. May God bless you and may our encounter create effective change.

God Bless,
Michelle Miles

Poem 1

Dear Mom

Written by Michelle Miles

Dear Mom, sorry I didn't obey your orders as a child.
Instead of listening to you, I chose to run wild.
You wanted nothing but the best for me.
But, I was caught up in the streets and could not see.
Now I sit alone in a prison cell.
My poor choices landed me to a place that is likened to hell.
Mom, I want to tell you just how I feel.
These people showed no mercy, I got such a raw deal!
I should have listened to you, because you were always right.
But somehow I got lost in the dark of the night.
I long for the day you will hold me in your arms.
Then I will feel protected from all hurt and harm.
I just wanted to drop a line and let you know I'm not dead.
I've been sentenced to 30 years; I'm "warehoused" in the FEDS.

Poem 2
Prisoner's Struggle

by Michelle Miles

Each day I awake, prison is my reality.
I'm locked up in a place with prisoners of every nationality.
I never thought in a million years that prison would be a part
of my fate.
But when I tried to change my lifestyle, I was just a little too
late.
Some get by, but others get caught.
There is no one to blame for our actions are our own fault.
All we can do is find ways to survive.
I'm so thankful to God that I am still alive.
When the agent's told me I was under arrest,
My heart nearly bust inside of my chest.
My incarceration was a message to me indeed.
It was God telling me to change my life and to take heed.
He said at the time you have fallen from My grace.
I had to save you by allowing you to come to such a place.
In the fiery furnace, I have learned many lessons.
Now I patiently await this season to change, so I can receive my
blessings.
Take heed to my story and know crime won't ever pay!
Consequences will always arise, even if its not right away.
Therefore, cherish your life and value your freedom.

And, reach for your goals, you surely can achieve them.
Never let anyone deter you from living your dreams.
Life isn't as bad as it may seem.
LOOK UP!

About the Author

MICHELLE MILES, born and raised in Brooklyn, New York, is currently a federal prisoner who is serving a 30 year sentence as a non-violent, drug offender. With 16 years of serving prison time under her belt, she has utilized her real-life experience to enlighten others to the true-life circumstances of women in prison and the dilemmas that they face in the U.S. judicial system. Miles is a modern day voice for women behind bars and prison reform in America.

Voices International Publications Presents

$\mathcal{V}oices$ of
CONSEQUENCES
ENRICHMENT SERIES
CREATED BY: JAMILA T. DAVIS

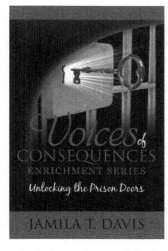

Unlocking the Prison Doors: 12 Points to Inner Healing and Restoration

ISBN: 978-09855807-4-2 Textbook
ISBN: 978-09855807-5-9 Workbook/Journal
ISBN: 978-09855807-6-6 Curriculum Guide

Unlocking the Prison Doors is a nondenominational, faith-based instructional manual created to help incarcerated women gain inner healing and restoration. In a comforting voice that readers can recognize and understand, this book provides the tools women need to get past the stage of denial and honestly assess their past behavioral patterns, their criminal conduct and its impact on their lives and others. It provides a platform for women to begin a journey of self-discovery, allowing them to assess the root of their problems and dilemmas and learn how to overcome them.

This book reveals real-life examples and concrete strategies that inspire women to release anger, fear, shame and guilt and embrace a new world of opportunities.

After reading *Unlocking the Prison Doors,* readers will be empowered to release the inner shackles and chains that have been holding them bound and begin to soar in life!

INTERNATIONAL PUBLICATIONS
"Changing Lives One Page At A Time."
www.vocseries.com

Voices International Publications Presents

$\mathcal{V}$oices of
CONSEQUENCES
ENRICHMENT SERIES
CREATED BY: JAMILA T. DAVIS

Permission to Dream:
12 Points to Discovering Your Life's Purpose and Recapturing Your Dreams

ISBN: 978-09855807-4-2 Textbook
ISBN: 978-09855807-5-9 Workbook/Journal
ISBN: 978-09855807-6-6 Curriculum Guide

Permission to Dream is a nondenominational, faith-based, instruction manual created to inspire incarcerated women to discover their purpose in life and recapture their dreams. In a way readers can identify with and understand, this book provides strategies they can use to overcome the stigma and barriers of being an ex-felon.

This book reveals universal laws and proven self-help techniques that successful people apply in their everyday lives. It helps readers identify and destroy bad habits and criminal thinking patterns, enabling them to erase the defilement of their past.

Step-by-step this book empowers readers to recognize their talents and special skill sets, propelling them to tap into the power of "self" and discover their true potential, and recapture their dreams.

After reading *Permission To Dream*, readers will be equipped with courage and tenacity to take hold of their dreams and become their very best!

INTERNATIONAL PUBLICATIONS
"Changing Lives One Page At A Time."
www.vocseries.com

Voices International Publications Presents

$\mathcal{V}oices$ of
CONSEQUENCES
ENRICHMENT SERIES
CREATED BY: JAMILA T. DAVIS

Pursuit to A Greater "Self:" 12 Points to Developing Good Character and HealthyRelationships

ISBN: 978-09855807-7-3 Textbook
ISBN: 978-09855807-8-0 Workbook/Journal
ISBN: 978-09855807-9-7 Curriculum Guide

Pursuit to A Greater "Self" is a non-denominational, faith-based, instruction manual created to help incarcerated women develop good character traits and cultivate healthy relationships.

This book is filled with real-life examples that illustrate how good character traits have helped many people live a more prosperous life, and how deficient character has caused others to fail. These striking examples, along with self-help strategies revealed in this book, are sure to inspire women to dethrone bad character traits and develop inner love, joy, peace, patience, kindness, generosity, faithfulness, gentleness and self-control. This book also instructs women how to utilize these positive character traits to cultivate healthy relationships.

After reading *Pursuit to A Greater "Self,"* readers will be inspired to let their light shine for the world to see that true reformation is attainable, even after imprisonment!

INTERNATIONAL PUBLICATIONS
"Changing Lives One Page At A Time."
www.vocseries.com

NOW AVAILABLE FROM

UOICES

INTERNATIONAL PUBLICATIONS

"Every negative choice we make in life comes with a consequence. Sometimes the costs we are forced to pay are severe!"
— Jamila T. Davis

She's All Caught Up is a real-life cautionary tale that exemplifies the powerful negative influences that affect today's youth and the consequences that arise from poor choices.

Young Jamila grew up in a loving middle class home, raised by two hardworking parents, the Davises, in the suburbs of Jamaica Queens, New York. Determined to afford their children the luxuries that they themselves never had, the Davises provided their children with a good life, hoping to guarantee their children's success.

At first it seemed as though their formula worked. Young Jamila maintained straight As and became her parents ideal "star child," as she graced the stage of Lincoln Center's Avery Fischer Hall in dance recitals and toured the country in a leading role in an off-Broadway play. All was copacetic in the Davis household until high school years when Jamila met her first love Craig- a 16 year old drug dealer from the Southside housing projects of Jamaica Queens.

As this high school teen rebels, breaking loose from her parents' tight reins, the Davises wage an "all-out" battle to save their only daughter whom they love so desperately. But Jamila is in too deep! Poisoned by the thorn of materialism, she lusts after independence, power and notoriety, and she chooses life in the fast lane to claim them.

When this good girl goes bad, it seems there is no turning back!
Follow author, Jamila T. Davis (creator of the Voices of Consequences Enrichment Series) in her trailblazing memoir, *She's All Caught Up!*

DECEMBER 2013
ISBN: 978-09855807-3-5
www.voicesbooks.com

COMING SOON!

The Trade Off

THE SEQUEL TO SHE'S ALL CAUGHT UP!

A MEMOIR

JAMILA T. DAVIS

ORDER FORM

Mail to: 196-03 Linden Blvd.
St. Albans, NY 11412
or visit us on the web @
www.vocseries.com

QTY	Title	Price
	Unlocking the Prison Doors	14.95
	Unlocking the Prison Doors Workbook/Journal	14.95
	Permission to Dream	14.95
	Permission to Dream Workbook/Journal	14.95
	Pursuit to A Greater "Self"	14.95
	Pursuit to A Greater "Self" Workbook/Journal	14.95
	The High Price I Had To Pay	7.99
	Total For Books	
	20% Inmate Discount -	
	Shipping/Handling +	
	Total Cost	

* Shipping/Handling 1-3 books 4.95
　　　　4-9 books 8.95
* Incarcerated individuals receive a 20% discount on each book purchase.
* Forms of Accepted Payments: Certified Checks, Institutional Checks and Money Orders.
* Bulk rates are available upon requests for orders of 10 books or more.
* Curriculum Guides are available for group sessions.
* All mail-in orders take 5-7 business days to be delivered. For prison orders, please allow
up to (3) three weeks for delivery.

SHIP TO:

Name: _____

Address: _____

_____

_____

City: _____

State: _____ Zip: _____

CPSIA information can be obtained at www.ICGtesting.com
Printed in the USA
BVOW10s1843180715

408829BV00005B/32/P